I0620454

The Reflection Journal Navigating Emotions

Faith and Feelings

Embracing Our Humanity

"Embracing emotions doesn't weaken our faith; instead, it helps us connect with our humanity and enriches our experiences as a person."

WRITTEN BY: ANNA L. WOODS, MMIN,
Trauma-informed Resilience Life & Grief Coach Certified
Navigating Life's Challenges

DISCLAIMER

How Journaling or Reflective Writing Helps

Journaling or reflective writing can be a powerful tool for personal growth and emotional well-being. It helps process thoughts and feelings and provides an outlet for expressing emotions that might be difficult to articulate otherwise. This practice encourages self-discovery, enhances clarity of thought, and can lead to greater emotional regulation. By writing about experiences or challenges, individuals often find solutions, gain new perspectives, and cultivate a sense of empowerment. Additionally, journaling can enhance mindfulness, allowing you to remain present and engaged with their thoughts.

How to Journal:

1. **Choose a Medium:** Decide whether you want to use a physical notebook, this journal or a digital platform. Select what feels most comfortable and accessible to you, handwritten journals have unique benefits. Enhancing the overall experience and fostering greater self-discovery.

2. **Set a Time:** Allocate specific times for journaling. This could be daily, weekly, or whenever you feel the need to express your thoughts.

3. **Find a Quiet Space:** Choose a location that feels peaceful and conducive to reflection, helping you concentrate without distractions.

4. **Begin with Prompts:** Start your journaling sessions with prompts provided here. This will involve reflecting on your emotions, or specific experiences.

5. **Write Freely:** Allow your thoughts to flow without self-editing. The goal is to express yourself authentically, so don't worry about grammar or structure.

Copyright

About The Author

Anna L. Woods is a dedicated Coaching Professional whose journey has been profoundly shaped by her personal experiences with grief and faith. With a Master's degree in Ministry and certifications as a Trauma-informed Resilience Coach, Life Coach, and Grief Coach, Anna has cultivated a rich tapestry of knowledge and empathy that fuels her mission to help others.

The loss of her beloved mother marked a pivotal turning point for Anna, casting her into a landscape of deep sorrow and prompting her to confront the profound questions of faith, healing, and resilience. Raised in a loving Christian household, Anna struggled to align her intense emotions with her upbringing, often reflecting on her father's words: "You got to know Jesus for yourself," and her mother's gentle encouragement, "You just keep living; you will understand someday." These teachings became the cornerstone of her understanding that faith and emotional challenges can coexist.

Anna's quest for understanding led her to pursue biblical education and further academic studies, uncovering the relationship between grief, trauma, and the body's response to emotional pain. Through her journey, she learned to recognize the physical manifestations of grief and how intentional awareness and coping strategies can transform overwhelming feelings into pathways for healing.

As the President of Navigating Life's Challenges (NLC), a nonprofit organization dedicated to emotional support and guidance, and as Vice President of Pro-Vets Group Inc., Anna utilizes her extensive background in leadership and human resources to empower individuals facing emotional difficulties. With over twenty-six years of experience in retail operations management, she possesses a unique insight into the complexities of human emotions within both personal and professional realms.

Holding a BA in Organizational Leadership and a Master's in Ministry and Strategic Leadership from Warner University, Anna is not just a coach; she is an advocate for those traversing the difficult terrain of grief. She actively participates in community outreach, hosting workshops and speaking at conferences focused on grief and mental wellness. Through her work, Anna L. Woods aims to illuminate the nuances of grief, offering hope and guidance to those navigating their emotional journeys in search of light amidst the darkness.

Dedication

Reflective Journal: "Faith & Feeling"
This journal is dedicated to my beloved parents, James E. May and Clara Knight May, both of whom are deceased. Together and individually, they bestowed upon me the invaluable gift of wisdom through their words: "You have to know Jesus for yourself." I can still hear Mama's encouraging voice reminding me, "Just keep living; you will understand someday."
These profound statements ignited a spark within me—a curiosity to explore my faith, learn, grow, and connect with others in the community. Their teachings have shaped my life in countless ways, and I aspire for their legacy of faith and understanding to endure for generations to come.

Acknowledgment

To my husband, thank you for your unwavering support as I pursue the person God intends for me to be.

To our blended, blessed, and cherished family of four adult children Jennifer, Darren Jr, Daniel and Danielle, and two wonderful granddaughters Samarie, and Sydney, I am grateful for each of you just being yourselves. When I asked you to share your thoughts on who I am as a Mom/Mums, your words touched my heart: "Mom, you are resilient, loving, faithful, graceful, whitty, persistent, understanding, and always caring. You are intentional, thoughtful, nurturing, reflective, supportive, kind, active, and intelligent."

To my entire family, every endeavor I undertake is fueled by a desire to grow into a better human being, sibling, mother, and wife. Thank you for your love and encouragement.

Dear Journal Keeper,

Welcome to "Faith and Feelings: Embracing Our Humanity." This journal is your sanctuary, a nurturing space dedicated to exploring the intricate landscape of your emotions as you navigate the profound journey of grief and healing.Grief in not just death but loss of any kind stiring a whirlwind of feelings—each valid and deserving of your attention.

This journal's purpose is to guide you in understanding and embracing these emotions, fostering a deeper connection with both your faith and your humanity. Remember, healing is not a linear process. As you engage with the prompts and reflections within these pages, expect to encounter a winding path filled with both ups and downs—and that's perfectly okay.

There are no strict timelines or definitive signs to guide your journey; each person's experience with grief is deeply personal and unfolds in its own unique way. Allow yourself the grace to embrace this journey, giving yourself the necessary space to grow and evolve. There is no right or wrong way to grieve—your path is distinctly yours, shaped by your emotions, memories, and the faith that sustains you.

I understand the struggle of how to "just give it to God." For years, I grappled with that comforting phrase while feeling the weight of overwhelming loss and grief. It's natural for those feelings to linger. In these pages, I hope you will discover your path forward through prayer and meditation, finding solace, encouragement, and inspiration.

As you embark on this reflective process, may you find comfort in the thoughtfully chosen words that lie ahead. May they inspire you to fully experience and understand the emotions that arise, enriching your journey toward healing and resilience.

With compassion and support,
Anna L. Woods, MMin

THE LORD IS MY SHEPARD I SHALL NOT WANT. PSALM 23:1

Table Of Content

Feeling Your Feelings

How do you differentiate between feelings and emotions?

Insight: Understanding the distinction can help you articulate your experiences more clearly.

"The heart is deceitful above all things and beyond cure. Who can understand it?" – Jeremiah 17:9

Navigating Life's Challenges
Exercise: Journaling Your Emotional Landscape

Write down three emotions you've felt today and describe what triggered them.

Reflect: Did you allow yourself to fully feel these emotions, or did you suppress them?

What specific feelings arise when you think about your loss?

Insight: Identifying specific feelings can assist in recognizing and working through your grief.

"The Lord is close to the brokenhearted and saves those who are crushed in spirit." – Psalm 34:18

Exercise: Emotional Check-In

Primary Emotions (e.g., sadness, anger, love)
Secondary Emotions (e.g., guilt, relief, regret)
Reflect: Which emotions dominate? Which ones surprise you?

_____

_____

_____

_____

_____

_____

_____

_____

_____

_____

_____

_____

_____

_____

Examine and define grief in your own words. What emotions are you feeling.

Insight: Defining grief in your own terms can help ground your emotions and experiences.

"Jesus wept." – John 11:35 (This simple verse acknowledges the depth of grief.)

Examining Emotions of Grief
Exercise: Letter to Your Grief

Write a letter to your grief as if it were a person.
Express how it has shaped you, what you've learned from it, and any unresolved thoughts you need to share.

How do you usually express your feelings?

Insight: Recognizing your methods of expression can lead to healthier communication and coping.

"A joyful heart is good medicine, but a crushed spirit dries up the bones." – Proverbs 17:22

Feeling Your Feelings
Exercise: Emotional Mapping

Create a mind map of your emotions. Start with your current mood in the center and branch out with words that describe your thoughts, physical sensations, and reactions.

Identify: Which emotions are dominant in your life? How do they influence your actions?

What emotions do you feel most often in your day-to-day life?

Insight: Understanding your emotional landscape can provide insight into your overall well-being.

"But the fruit of the Spirit is love, joy, peace, forbearance, kindness, goodness, faithfulness, gentleness, and self-control." – Galatians 5:22-23

Exercise: Naming the Feeling

Choose one emotion that stands out the most when you think about your loss.

Describe what it feels like in your body (e.g., "Sadness feels like a weight on my chest.").

What thoughts come with this emotion? How do they affect your actions?

Impact of Grief

When you experience grief, what physical sensations do you notice in your body?

Insight: Recognizing physical symptoms can help you connect emotions with bodily reactions.

My life is consumed by anguish and my years by groaning; my strength fails because of my affliction, and my bones grow weak." – Psalm 31:10

Impact of Grief
Exercise: Body Awareness Meditation

Sit in a quiet place, close your eyes, and focus on where grief manifests in your body
(e.g., chest tightness, stomach discomfort).
Write about the sensations and any memories or emotions they bring up.

What emotions do you believe society encourages you to suppress?

Insight: Acknowledging societal pressures can empower you to embrace a fuller range of emotions.

"Rejoice with those who rejoice; mourn with those who mourn."
– Romans 12:15

Going Deeper Reflective Practice
Exercise: Walking Meditation on Emotions

Take a 10-minute walk in silence.
With each step, name an emotion you're currently holding onto and visualize it releasing with each breath.
Afterward, journal about how you felt before and after.

Going Deeper Reflective Practice
Exercise: Walking Meditation on Emotions

What role do you think feeling your feelings and emotions play in a person's ability to heal from grief?

Insight: Exploring this connection can guide you in integrating emotions into your healing process

----

"He heals the brokenhearted and binds up their wounds."
— Psalm 147:3

Exercise: Drawing Your Emotions

Using colors, symbols, or even simple doodles, illustrate the emotions tied to your loss. You don't need to be an artist—just visually express what words may not fully capture. Reflect: Did you notice any hidden emotions while drawing?

Reflect on how your understanding of emotions has evolved over time.

Insight: Growth in understanding can enhance your ability to navigate your emotional landscape.

"In all your ways acknowledge Him, and He will make your paths straight."
– Proverbs 3:6

A Journey of Self-Understanding and Connection
Exercise: The Mirror Talk

Stand in front of a mirror and Read out loud, "I acknowledge my grief.
I allow myself to feel. I honor my journey."
Write about how it felt to say these words and what emotions arose.

What have you learned about the relationship between feelings, emotions, and faith in your life?

Insight: Exploring this relationship can deepen your understanding of how faith can support your emotional health.

"Now faith is confidence in what we hope for and assurance about what we do not see." – Hebrews 11:1

Understanding Your Grief: Emotional Exploration
Exercise: Faith and Emotion Integration

Read a passage of scripture that speaks about grief.
Write how this scripture applies to your current emotional state.
How does faith provide comfort in your journey?

What emotions do you associate with your grief journey?

Insight: Emotions are valid and serve as a guide to understanding your grief.

Scripture: "Jesus wept." – John 11:35

Exercise: Talking to Your Loss

Write a letter to the person or thing you lost, expressing the emotions that come up when you think about them.
If your emotions had a voice, what would they say?

Examining the Emotions of Grief

How can acknowledging your emotions enhance your relationship with others?

Insight: Sharing your feelings fosters deeper connection and empathy.

"Bear one another's burdens, and so fulfill the law of Christ."
– Galatians 6:2

Going Deeper
Reflective
Practice

How has exploring your feelings and grief enhanced your self-understanding and connection to others? Reflect on how this awareness influences your faith, healing journey, and relationships.

Read John 11:33-37. Reflect on Jesus' emotions and how they relate to your humanity.

Exercise: The Mirror of Grief

Write about how grief has changed your self-perception.
What have you learned about your emotional strength and vulnerabilities?
How has this self-awareness shaped the way you connect with others?

Read John 11:33-37. Reflect on Jesus' emotions and how they
relateto your humanity.

How have past experiences with emotions shaped your current grief?

Insight: Reflecting on the past can illuminate how you've grown through emotional challenges.

"And we know that in all things God works for the good of those who love him. – Romans 8:28

Exercise: Emotional Timeline

Draw a timeline of key emotional experiences in your life, marking moments of significant joy, sadness, loss, or resilience.
Identify patterns: How have past experiences influenced the way you navigate grief today?
Reflect: What emotional strengths have you developed over time?

What comfort do you find in your faith during times of emotional turmoil?

Insight: Leaning into your faith can provide solace amid emotional upheaval.

"Cast all your anxiety on him because he cares for you."
— 1 Peter 5:7

Exercise: Guided Breathing for Emotional Awareness

Close your eyes and take slow, deep breaths.
With each inhale, name the emotion you feel.
With each exhale, imagine gently releasing tension from your body.
After five minutes, journal about any emotional shifts you noticed.

Exercise: Guided Breathing for Emotional Awareness

"The Lord is near to the brokenhearted and saves the crushed in spirit." – Psalm 34:18

Exercise: The Emotional Lens

Think about a past grief or emotional challenge. How did you respond then compared to now?
Then: How did you process emotions in the past?
Now: How do you process them differently?
What lessons have helped you navigate your current grief with more self-awareness?

How can recognizing your emotions improve your coping strategies?

Insight: Understanding your emotional responses can lead to healthier coping mechanisms.

"Be strong and take heart, all you who hope in the Lord."
— Psalm 31:24

Exercise: Letter to Your Younger Self

Write a letter to a younger version of yourself during a time of past grief or emotional hardship.
Offer words of encouragement, acknowledging the growth and strength you have now.
Reflect: How would your younger self view your resilience today?

What tools or practices help you process difficult emotions?

Insight: Exploring various methods such as journaling, coaching, therapy, or meditation can aid in emotional processing.

"My soul finds rest in God alone; my salvation comes from him."
– Psalm 62:1

Reflect on a Past Hurt

Write about how you feel and what forgiveness means in this context.

Insight:

Reflecting on a specific past hurt allows you to identify emotions tied to that experience. Acknowledging these feelings can be the first step toward emotional release and healing.

Ephesians 4:31-32 – "Get rid of all bitterness, rage, anger, harsh words, and slander, as well as all types of evil behavior. Instead, be kind to each other, tenderhearted, forgiving one another, just as God through Christ has forgiven you."

Holding On
Describe the Emotions Associated with Holding a Grudge

Insight:

Grudges can often cloud your judgment and create a cycle of negativity. By exploring the emotions linked to holding onto resentment, you can understand its weight and recognize the mental clarity that forgiveness can provide.

Matthew 6:14-15 – "If you forgive those who sin against you, your heavenly Father will forgive you. But if you refuse to forgive others, your Father will not forgive your sins."

Forgiving others and Yourself

Write About Someone You Need to Forgive, this can also be about you. Consider, we often need to forgive ourselves first, showing compassion for the things we did not know or understand.

Insight:

Identifying someone you need to forgive can empower you to take the first steps toward releasing your anger. Reflect on how forgiving this person or yourself) could restore your sense of control and promote your emotional well-being.

Colossians 3:13 – "Make allowance for each other's faults, and forgive anyone who offends you. Remember, the Lord forgave you, so you must forgive others."

Explore How Forgiveness Can Lead to Inner Peace

Write about the potential for inner peace once you have forgiven others.
What would that feel like? How would it change your perspective?

Insight:

Forgiveness can create space for healing and peace. Write about the potential for inner peace in your life once you have forgiven others.

----

2 Corinthians 1:3-4 – "All praise to God, the Father of our Lord Jesus Christ. God is our merciful Father and the source of all comfort. He comforts us in all our troubles, so that we can comfort others."

Letting Go

Make a list of how letting go of anger could improve your mental and physical health.

Insight:

Exploring the benefits of emotional release can help you see forgiveness as a pathway to personal empowerment and stress reduction.

Scriptural Support: Proverbs 19:11 – "Sensible people control their tempers; they earn respect by overlooking wrongs."

Reflect on Empathy and Compassion Towards Others

Write about how gaining perspective on someone's situation could lead to greater compassion and healing.

Insight:

Forgiveness nurtures empathy, helping to foster understanding of others' complexities. Write about how gaining perspective on someone's situation could lead to greater compassion and healing in your life.

Luke 6:36 – "You must be compassionate, just as your Father is compassionate."

Consider the Cycle of Pain in Unforgiveness

Write about how forgiving can help you move forward and promote healthier interactions.

Insight:

Reflecting on the consequences of unforgiveness helps break the cycle of pain that impacts current and future relationships. Write about how forgiving can help you move forward and promote healthier interactions.

Matthew 7:1-2 – "Do not judge others, and you will not be judged. For you will be treated as you treat others. The standard you use in judging is the standard by which you will be judged."

Envision Your Life After Forgiveness

Describe what that life looks like—how you interact with others, the
feelings you experience, and the freedom you gain.

Envision Your Life After Forgiveness

Philippians 4:7 – "Then you will experience God's peace, which exceeds anything we can understand. His peace will guard your hearts and minds as you live in Christ Jesus."

Exercise: Emotional Patterns Journal

Over the next few days, journal when you notice grief surfacing.
Reflect on the difference these moments to past emotional experiences.
What triggers remain the same? What has changed in your ability to cope?

A Journey of Self-Understanding and Connection

What role does vulnerability play in your healing process?

Insight: Being vulnerable can open doors to support and understanding.

Exercise: Identifying Emotional Growth

List three ways your past emotional experiences have shaped how you handle grief today
Identify one coping strategy you've gained from past challenges that is helping you now
Write about how your emotional responses have evolved.

"My grace is sufficient for you, for my power is made perfect in weakness.
Therefore I will boast all the more gladly about my weaknesses, so that
Christ's power may rest on me."– 2 Corinthians 12:9

How has your perspective on love changed since your loss?

Insight: Grief often deepens our understanding and appreciation for love's enduring nature.

"And now these three remain: faith, hope, and love.
But the greatest of these is love."
1 Corinthians 13:13

Exercise: Love Before & After

Divide a page into two columns:
Before Loss: How did you view love before your loss?
After Loss: How do you see love now?
Reflect: What has deepened or shifted in your understanding of love's role
in your life?

Reflect on how you can incorporate your loved one's memory into your life.

Insight: Keeping memories alive can provide comfort and connection amidst grief.

"A good name is better than fine perfume,"
— Ecclesiastes 7:1

Exercise: Love Letters to the Past & Present

Write two short letters:
One to the person (or thing) you lost, expressing how they shaped your view of love.
One to yourself, recognizing how grief has transformed your ability to give and receive love.
What new realizations emerge from this exercise?

Exercise: Love Letters to the Past & Present

What fears around grief do you need to confront?

Insight: Confronting fears can empower you and pave the way for healing.

"For I am the Lord your God who takes hold of your right hand and says to you, Do not fear; I will help you." – Isaiah 41:13

Exercise: Love's Presence in Loss

Reflect on the ways love still exists despite your loss.
List five ways love continues to manifest in your life (e.g., memories,
relationships, self-compassion, faith).
How does recognizing love's presence shift your grief?

Understanding Your Grief: Emotional Exploration

How has your understanding of grief evolved through exploring your feelings and emotions, and what new insights have you gained about the relationship between your grief and your faith?

Insight: Self-care in grief means prioritizing well-being, seeking support, and being gentle as I navigate my emotions and heal.

Exercise: Acts of Love Journal

For a week, write down small ways you express or receive love each day.
How does grief influence the way you appreciate these moments?
What does love look like to you now?

Celebrate

How can you celebrate small victories in your healing journey?
Insight: Acknowledging progress, no matter how small, can enhance your
sense of hope.

"Let everything that has breath praise the Lord!"
— Psalm 150:6

Celebrate
Exercise: Gratitude Journal for Healing

List three small victories you have achieved in your healing journey.
Reflect: How has each step brought you closer to peace?

What does it mean for you to embrace vulnerability in your faith?
Insight: Embracing vulnerability can strengthen your faith and relationships with others.

"God is our refuge and strength, an ever-present help in trouble." – Psalm 46:1

Exercise: Love & Legacy

Think about how the love you shared with the one you lost continues to impact you.
How can you honor that love moving forward?
Write about one action you can take to carry that love into the future.

Write about how your grief has changed your view on human connection.

Insight: Grief can deepen your understanding of the importance of relationships and community.

"We are many parts of one body, and we all depend oneach other."
— 1 Corinthians 12:27

Exercise: The Role of Others in Your Healing

Make a list of people who have supported you during your grief journey.
Reflect: How has their presence or absence shaped your understanding of
relationships?
What have you learned about the role of community in healing?

Going Deeper:
Exploring the Emotions of Jesus

John 15:11
John 13:34
Matthew 21:12
Luke 22: 39-46
Luke 22:42
Matthew 26:50
Matthew 9:36
Jesus Wept: John 11:35
Matthew 26:38-40

In what ways do you feel faith and emotions can coexist?

Insight: Acknowledging that faith can support emotional experiences fosters resilience.

"The Spirit himself intercedes for us through wordless groans."
— Romans 8:26

"The Spirit himself intercedes for us through wordless groans."
— Romans 8:26

"The Spirit himself intercedes for us through wordless groans."
– Romans 8:26

Exercise: Connection Then & Now

Write about how you viewed relationships before your loss versus now.
Do you value certain connections more deeply? Have your priorities in
relationships changed?
How has grief influenced the way you communicate with others?

Embracing Our Humanity

What emotions do you find difficult to express, and how can Jesus' willingness to express His feelings inspire you to share your own?
Insight: Understanding that Jesus openly expressed His emotions gives us permission to do the same, promoting healing through authenticity.

"My soul is overwhelmed with sorrow to the point of death."
– Matthew 26:38

Exercise: A Letter of Gratitude

Write a heartfelt letter to someone who has been there for you during your grief.
You don't have to send it—just reflect on how their support has affected you.
What does this letter reveal about your evolving perspective on human connection?

In what ways do you see Jesus reflecting the breadth of human emotions during His time on Earth?
Insight: Recognizing that Jesus experienced a full range of emotions allows us to understand that feeling deeply is a part of being human.

"Jesus wept." – John 11:35

Exercise: The Gift of Empathy

Think of a time when you comforted someone else who was grieving.
How did your own grief shape the way you showed up for them?
Reflect on how loss has made you more attuned to others' pain and needs.

How does the understanding that Jesus experienced grief impact your own grieving process?

Insight: Knowing that Jesus grieved can provide comfort and validation for your own feelings of loss, showing that grief is a shared human experience.

"And when he drew near and saw the city, he wept over it."
– Luke 19:41

Exercise: The People Who Understand

Write about a moment when someone truly understood your grief without needing to fix it.
What did they say or do that made you feel seen and supported?
How can you offer that kind of presence to others?

Reflect on a time when you felt empathy toward someone else's pain. How does Jesus' example influence your ability to empathize with others?

Insight: Jesus' compassion for others encourages us to be present with those in grief, fostering connection and support.

"When he saw the crowds, he had compassion for them, because they were harassed and helpless, like sheep without a shepherd."
– Matthew 9:36

Exercise: A Moment of Shared Pain

Write about a time when you deeply felt someone else's suffering.
What emotions arose within you?
How did you respond—through words, actions, or silent presence?

How can embracing the emotional experiences of Jesus help you feel more empowered to navigate your own grief?

Insight: Recognizing Jesus' journey through emotional pain can inspire resilience and encourage you to honor your own feelings as valid and meaningful.

"In this world, you will have trouble. But take heart! I have overcome the world." – John 16:33

Exercise: Walking in Their Shoes

Imagine yourself in the place of the person who was hurting.
How do you think they felt in that moment?
What would you have wanted from others if you were in their situation?

Resilience Through Emotion

How can acknowledging and expressing your feelings during tough times strengthen your resilience?

Insight: Embracing your feelings allows for emotional release and healing, which is vital for building resilience.

"Blessed are those who mourn, for they will be comforted."
– Matthew 5:4

Resilience Through Emotion

How can acknowledging and expressing your feelings during tough times strengthen your resilience?

Exercise: The Strength in Vulnerability

Write about a time when you allowed yourself to express difficult emotions instead of suppressing them.

How did it feel in the moment?

Looking back, how did that experience contribute to your emotional growth?

Resilience Through Emotion

Reflect on a past emotional challenge that helped you grow stronger. What feelings did you embrace during that time?

Insight: Embracing difficult feelings can lead to personal growth and a deeper understanding of yourself.

"Consider it pure joy, my brothers and sisters, whenever you face trials of many kinds." – James 1:2

Exercise: Naming & Releasing Emotions

Identify three emotion you are currently struggling with. Write them down and describe how they react your thoughts and body. Next, write a release statement (e.g., I acknowledge my sadness, and I allow myself to feel it without judgment). React: How does puttng words to your emotion help light the burden?

In what ways can finding meaning in your grief help you cultivate resilience?

Insight: Recognizing the lessons learned from grief can empower you, giving purpose to your pain.

"I know that you can do all things; no purpose of yours can be thwarted." – Job 42:2

Exercise: Jesus' Emotional Resilience

Read about a moment when Jesus expressed emotion during hardship (e.g., in the Garden of Gethsemane – Luke 22:42-44).

Reflect: How did His willingness to express His pain give Him the strength to move forward?

How does His example encourage you to face difficult emotions with courage?

Embracing Humanity

In what ways can the emotional experiences of Jesus inspire you to embrace your own feelings and deepen your connections with others as you navigate your grief and life's ongoing emotional challenges?

Sharing our story can be a healing act, offering support and hope to others who grieve, while honoring our own journey through pain.

Embracing Our Humanity
Exercise: Lessons from Jesus

Read a passage where Jesus expresses emotion (e.g., John 11:35).
Write about how Jesus' emotions give you permission to feel and express your own.

The Reflection Journal Navigating Emotions

What will you do differently with what you have experienced and learn through this journey?

Exercise: A Letter to Your Future Self

Write a letter to yourself one year from now.
Acknowledge where you are in your healing journey today and express hope
for how you will continue to grow.
What do you want your future self to remember about this experience?

"You have faith; I have deeds.Show me your faith without deeds, and I will show you my faith by my deeds." —James 2:18

Dear Journal Keeper

As you reach the final pages of this journal, I invite you to pause and reflect on th transformative path you have traveled. Through each reflection and emotional exploratior you have courageously navigated the intricate landscape of your feelings. These emotion often complex and overwhelming, are not barriers to overcome but essential threads tha weave together the fabric of your humanity. Embracing them is an act of profoun strength—one that nurtures resilience and fosters deeper connections with yourself an those around you.

Grief, while undeniably challenging, has also been a gateway to self-discovery an growth. Each entry you've penned stands as a testament to your vulnerability—not as sign of weakness, but as a wellspring of courage that empowers you to face life's uncertaintie with authenticity and grace. Let the insights and lessons you've uncovered within thes pages continue to guide you, reminding you that healing is not a destination but an ongoin journey.

As you close this chapter, may your heart remain open to the richness of your emotions i every facet of life. Treasure the connections you have nurtured, and welcome each da with compassion for yourself, allowing your feelings to be your compass. Remembe every emotion you acknowledge and embrace adds depth to your spirit and enriches you humanity. This journey does not end here; it will continue to unfold with every momer you allow yourself to feel, heal, and grow.

Thank you for allowing me to walk beside you on this reflective journey. My hope is tha you find lasting peace, unwavering strength, and a faith that carries you forward, full embracing the beautiful complexity of being human.

With Heartfelt Blessings,
Anna L. Woods

Coping strategies references:

1.Reduce Stress:
Pennebaker, J. W., & Chung, C. K. (2011). "Expressive writing: An inhibitory process." Psychological Science, 22(3), 325-331. doi:10.1177/0956797611400093

2.Increase Self-Esteem:
Emmons, R. A., & McCullough, M. E. (2003). "Counting blessings versus burdens: An experimental investigation of gratitude and subjective well-being in daily life." Journal of Personality and Social Psychology, 84(2), 377-389. doi:10.1037/0022-3514.84.2.377

3.Reduce Blood Pressure:
Smyth, J. M. (1998). "Written emotional expression: effect sizes, impact on health, and revelations." Health Psychology, 17(3), 253-264. doi:10.1037/0278-6133.17.3.253

4.Improve Decision-Making:
Lepper, M. R., & Greene, D. (1978). "Turning children into temporary/community leads: The effects of rewards on intrinsic motivation." Journal of Personality and Social Psychology, 28(1), 582-590. doi:10.1037/h0034040

5.Decrease Levels of Anxiety and Depression:
Frattaroli, J. (2006). "Experimental disclosure and its moderat meta-analysis." Journal of Clinical Psychology, 62(6), 761-775. doi:10.1002/jclp.20212

www.ingramcontent.com/pod-product-compliance
Lightning Source LLC
Chambersburg PA
CBHW051222120626
46547CB00013B/1466